The Plants We Eat

**By Millicent E. Selsam
and Jerome Wexler**

The Amazing Dandelion

The Apple and Other Fruits

Bulbs, Corms, and Such

Eat the Fruit, Plant the Seed

The Harlequin Moth, Its Life Story

Maple Tree

Mimosa, The Sensitive Plant

Peanut

Play With Plants

Popcorn

Vegetables From Stems and Leaves

The Plants We Eat

Millicent E. Selsam

**PHOTOGRAPHS
BY JEROME WEXLER
AND OTHERS**

NEWLY REVISED EDITION

New York 1981 | William Morrow and Company

Photo Credits

All photographs are by Jerome Wexler with the exception of the following:
The American Museum of Natural History, pp. 86, 117; California Fig Institute, Research Laboratory, p. 106; Ferry Morse Seed Co., pp. 50, 51, 62;
Florida Citrus Commission, p. 100; The Metropolitan Museum of Art, pp. 12,
15 (Gift of Nathan Cummings, 1964), 36 (Gift of Nathan Cummings, 1964);
United Nations, pp. 59 (John Isaac, photographer), 96, 103 (FAO/S. Bunnag),
108, 109 (J. Frank, photographer); U.S. Department of Agriculture, pp. 18
(Soil Conservation Service, Robert L. Kane, photographer), 53 left, 54, 56,
66 top, 67, 78 both, 79 both, 95 (Soil Conservation Service), 101, 102 (Forest
Service), 105 (U.S. Date and Citrus Station), 115 all. Permission is gratefully
acknowledged.

Library of Congress Cataloging in Publication Data

Selsam, Millicent Ellis, 1912-
    Plants we eat.
    Summary: Discusses the development of the most common food plants, and
their changing uses. Includes simple directions for growing some of the plants
at home.
    1. Food crops—Juvenile literature.   [1. Plants, Edible.   2. Food crops]
I. Wexler, Jerome, ill. II. Title.
SB175.S44   1981   635   81-9450
ISBN 0-688-00719-8   AACR2
ISBN 0-688-00720-1 (lib. bdg.)

Contents

The Plants We Eat

1 | People and Plants

We eat plants every day. We walk into a store and buy potatoes and onions, beans and tomatoes. We eat bread that comes from wheat and breakfast cereals that were once grains growing in fields of corn or oats or rice. We eat luscious fruits picked from trees, vines, and bushes. Our salads are made of the crisp green leaves of plants.

But our prehistoric ancestors did not have such an easy time getting their food. They had to hunt animals and gather wild plants. For hundreds of thousands of years, they experimented with all the plants they found, tasting the leaves of one, the roots of another. They tried out berries and fruits and seeds. They learned which tasted good and which were bitter. They learned which plants kept them healthy and which made them sick.

All during this period, our prehistoric ancestors merely gathered food. It was thousands of years before they realized the importance of seeds. They did not know that if you sowed a seed in the ground, it would sprout into a new plant. Nobody knows just when or where or how people finally learned to grow plants themselves. All we know is that they did begin to sow seeds and to protect the growing plant until it could be used as food. This purposeful raising of plants started only about twelve thousand years ago.

The beginning of agriculture was the beginning of civilization. People began to settle down in one place to grow their own food; they began to live in groups and to build cities. Gradually, as people learned to cultivate the land, they also found time to make pottery, to paint, to develop writing and the calendar.

The first great civilizations depended on wheat. Charred remains of wheat have been found in Asia on the sites of villages twelve thousand years old in the Tigris Euphrates Valley of Mesopotamia, as well as in Southeast Asia. In caves in Southeast Asia there was evidence that peas, beans, and almonds were being cultivated in addition to wheat.

Egyptian wall painting of wheat harvest, from approximately 1415 B.C.

On the other side of the world, in Mexico and Central America, archaeologists (scientists who study the material remains of a country) have found that corn, beans, and squash were being cultivated five thousand years ago.

When we study the history of our food plants, we also learn a great deal about the history of people, for both developed together. In fact, every single food plant of any importance to us today was discovered by our prehistoric ancestors.

As soon as people began raising plants, they also began to improve them by saving the best seeds for planting the next year. For centuries, people all over the world have practiced this custom. We still do so today. For example, it is a harvest custom in Mexico to gather the best ears of corn from different fields and preserve them in a special granary for the next year's sowing.

As a result, most of our food plants changed. Spindly, unhealthy plants were weeded out; slowly the edible parts of each plant were developed until they became juicier, sweeter, and tastier. Many of them now also look quite different from the way they did in ancient times.

The practice of growing plants for food spread all over the world. People traveled. They moved from one country to another. They crossed rivers and mountains, and they took along with them the plants they had learned to use for food. As they mixed with other peoples, they found out about plants used in other parts of the world. They exchanged seeds. It is no wonder that tracing the early history of our food plants is difficult. Most plants were scattered through all the known lands of the earth long before there were written records to tell about them.

Botanists—plant scientists—have learned a great deal about man's first food plants, however, by adding one small clue to another. When all the pieces of information they discover about a plant fit together, they begin to see a whole picture, just as we do when we work a jigsaw puzzle. Sometimes they can eventually trace the whole history of a plant.

Some clues are dug out of the earth. Archaeologists have uncovered buried cities of long ago and have opened tombs and pyramids. They have found inscriptions that describe food plants and sculpture and paintings that picture them. Often they found remains of the plants themselves.

Plant scientists have also searched the classical literature of the Greeks and Romans looking for references to plants and have pored over the writings and carvings of ancient Egypt, Babylonia, China, and India. They have examined books of travel and exploration to find whether the author-explorer mentioned any plants.

Sometimes the names of plants help unravel their history. The word *tomato*, for instance, can be traced back to the Mexican Indian word *tomati*. Most of the names for cabbage—*capuccio* in Italian, cabbage in English—can be traced to the Latin word for head, *caput*. By tracing the spread of this word through Europe, we have learned a little more about the history of cabbage. But language clues are not always dependable. They have to be checked against other evidence.

The clearest clue to a plant's history is the discovery of a place where its ancestor is still growing wild. Nobody can question the origin of asparagus, for example, because the wild ancestor of this plant is still growing in eastern Mediterranean countries.

Peruvian vessel with squash design, from approximately A.D. 200–300

Plant explorers have gone on plant-hunting expeditions to the far corners of the world looking for the wild ancestors of some of our food plants. They have tramped through steaming forests, climbed high mountains, and searched plains in remote countries. Sometimes they found what they were looking for. As recently as the 1920's, the wild rela-

People and Plants | 15

tives of the white potato were found growing in western South America. This important evidence helped to clear up the history of the potato.

We learn about the history of plants in all these ways, but one bit of evidence alone is not enough. When all the clues gathered from archaeology, the study of language, plant exploration, written records, and plant breeding agree, we feel that we know most of the story of a plant. Usually we know only a part of the story and get just a glimpse into the past history of our food plants.

The
Roots
We
2 | Eat

All through history, people have dug up the underground parts of plants and eaten those that tasted good. We still do. We dig up and eat the roots of carrots, radishes, turnips, beets, parsnips, and sweet potatoes.

Like all plants, these plants manufacture food in their leaves for the plant to use, but they manufacture a lot more than the plant needs to live and grow. The extra food moves down to the underground roots where it is stored, and so carrots and radishes and turnips and beets and parsnips and sweet potatoes make good food for us.

All of these plants, except sweet potatoes, are biennials, which means they need two years to produce seeds. The first year they develop roots, stem, and leaves that manufacture the extra food later stored below the ground. But no flowers or seeds form on the plant. If the plant stays in the ground, the extra food in the root is a ready-made supply of nourishment for the next spring when the plant pushes up a flowering stalk.

We rarely see the flower stalks of these plants, because we are only interested in the edible roots that form the first year. But we cannot grow more plants unless we have seeds

harvesting carrot seed

to plant a new crop. Where do we get them? Most of the carrot and parsnip and turnip and beet and radish seed used in this country is produced in the valleys of California, where it is warm enough to grow crops even in winter. Usually the seed is sown in July, and by December the plant has completed its first-year growth. The roots are pulled up and the tops removed. Then the best roots are planted again. By the following June, the fields are in bloom, and by September the seeds are ripe. In this way, the growth of biennial plants is rushed so that they flower in one year. Radishes are brought to seed even faster. They are sown in December, and the seeds are ready to be harvested by the following September.

You can have fun watching the underground roots of these plants grow. Try the seeds of carrot, radish, parsnip, turnip, or beet. Sow them in a container, which may be an ordinary clay or plastic flowerpot. Use sterile potting soil, which you can buy in a five-and-ten or at a flower or garden shop. Plant the seeds and cover them lightly with a quarter inch of soil. When the tiny plants show above the ground, thin them out so there is an inch between each plant.

If you use radish seed you can watch the whole show. Pull up one of the plants every week, and you will see how the underground root grows bigger and bigger until you have a radish ready to eat! If you keep one radish plant

radish root developing

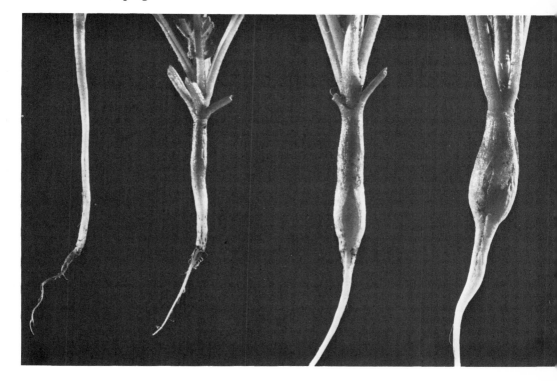

radish flower

growing for more than six months, it will flower and produce seeds. The other plants are too big to grow in a flowerpot very long, but you can enjoy seeing the early stages of their growth. One kind of carrot is an exception. It is called Tiny Sweet and can grow to full size in a flowerpot.

A plump carrot, radish, turnip, parsnip, or beet is very much alive. You can prove this easily by planting one of them in a flowerpot containing ordinary sterile potting soil. Lovely green leaves will soon grow out of the root, just as they do when these roots are planted in the field for a crop of seeds. You can even grow a new plant by cutting off the top two inches of the root and setting it in a dish of water. The new leaves of turnips and beets are very tender. They are delicious to eat in salads or cooked like spinach.

carrot top sprouting

If you should ever see a carrot plant in bloom, you might think you were looking at Queen Anne's lace. The lovely, branched flowering stalks of carrots and Queen Anne's lace are hard to tell apart, a sure sign that the plants belong to the same family. These two plants are very closely related; in fact, some people say that the carrot we eat came from Queen Anne's lace, which is also called wild carrot. Queen Anne's lace has a long root that looks like a carrot, but it is woody and tough rather than tender and sweet.

carrot flowers

More than a hundred years ago, some scientists planted Queen Anne's lace in good, well-fertilized garden soil and tended it carefully. After three years of replanting the seeds of the plants with the fleshiest roots, they reported that the wild carrot produced roots as fleshy and as large as those of the garden carrot. Other scientists think that this experiment is not enough proof. They feel that a lot more work has to be done before we can be sure that Queen Anne's lace is the ancestor of our carrot.

Queen Anne's lace

carrot root forming

Possibly both wild carrot and our cultivated carrot came from a primitive form of carrot that is still growing wild in Afghanistan in Middle Asia. Long, long ago some of these plants were carried to Asia Minor and from there to other Mediterranean countries, where our garden carrot developed. We know that the Greeks and Romans ate carrots, because they wrote about them. They thought they were

good for the stomach. Today we know that even though carrots may not cure stomach ailments they are good for our health, because they are rich sources of vitamin A. As centuries passed, carrots spread all over Europe and the rest of the world. They were brought to this country by the first American settlers. American Indians liked them too; the Iroquois were growing carrots two hundred years ago.

turnip root forming

Turnips, beets, and radishes have ancient histories too. The offerings the Greeks made to their god Apollo included turnips modeled in lead, beets in silver, and radishes in pure gold!

Radishes originated in China and spread from there to the rest of the world. Some of the radishes still grown in China and Japan today are two feet long! Japanese and Chinese people eat these huge radishes practically every day, either fresh or pickled the way we pickle cucumbers.

Turnips have also been known in Asia and Europe for many centuries. Every single part of the turnip can be eaten. Turnip roots are baked or boiled and mashed. The young shoots are used in salad, and the leaves are cooked like spinach. They are rich sources of vitamins and minerals.

A turnip grows like a radish or a carrot. The first year the turnip root gets bigger and bigger while only leaves form above the ground. The turnips are harvested at this stage.

During the second year of its growth, a turnip plant produces flowers. Seed pods form from the flowers.

turnip flowers

turnip seed pods

The ancestor of the beet—the sea beet—still grows along the Mediterranean coasts of southern Europe. It has a tough, woody, slender root that is not at all like the beet root we know, but the leaves look like beet leaves and can be eaten. Long ago the leaves were the only part of the plant that was gathered for food. Then someone found sea beets with large and fleshy roots and began to cultivate them. Hundreds of years passed, though, before beet roots were commonly used as a vegetable.

Beets also grow like carrots, radishes, and turnips. The first year the underground beet root forms. The beets are picked at this stage.

To get seeds, the best beets are kept in cold storage over the winter and planted in the spring. The second year both leaves and flowers form.

beet roots forming

beet plant

beet plant in flower

While people in Europe and Asia were munching on turnips and beets and carrots and radishes, they knew nothing of another root plant that grew only on the American continent. Not until Columbus first landed on the islands of the West Indies did Europeans find out about this delectable yellow root—the sweet potato.

The sweet potato is an underground storage root too, but there is a difference between it and the roots of carrots, beets, turnips, and radishes. One carrot or beet, if planted, will produce only one plant with flowers and seeds; but one sweet potato will grow several new sweet potato plants.

When a sweet potato is placed in warm, moist soil, it produces many buds. From each bud a new sweet potato plant sprouts.

In this country we grow our sweet potatoes from these sprouts. The farmer places sweet potato roots in warm, moist sand. Soon sprouts appear above the ground, and in about six weeks they are big enough to transplant to the fields. There are so many sprouts from each root that a farmer can grow about two thousand new plants from one bushel of sweet potato roots!

You can plant a sweet potato root the way commercial planters do. First, be sure to get a sweet potato that can grow. Many of the sweet potatoes in the stores have been dried out in ovens to keep them from spoiling. This treatment also keeps them from sprouting, so ask your vegetable man to find one that has some signs of life. If you can see buds on it and if there are some roots hanging from it, it will probably be a good root to plant.

Lay the potato horizontally on moist sand in a big flowerpot, and cover it with one inch of sand. Water the

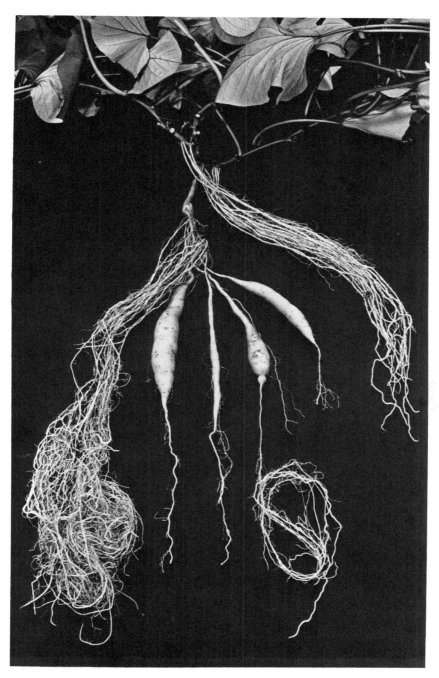

sweet potato roots forming

sand so that it is moist but not soaking wet. Within three weeks you will see the sprouts aboveground. As the sprout grows, sweet potato roots form under the ground. When the sprouts are six inches high, take the sweet potato out of the ground, pull off the sprouts one by one, and plant them in separate flowerpots containing ordinary potting soil. Don't worry about tearing some roots; the sprouts will form new roots quickly when you transplant them. The sweet potato, put back in the sand, will keep on sending up more sprouts. Plant those, too! See how many sweet potato plants you can get from one sweet potato root.

Sweet potato vines growing in the United States do not usually produce flowers and seeds, but in moist, hot climates the vines become covered with pink or purple blossoms that look very much like small morning glories. Here again the resemblance of the flowers shows that the plants are related. The sweet potato belongs to the morning glory family. Many plants in this family have swollen, sugary roots; but only the sweet potato has roots so big and sweet that the Indians in America noticed them long ago and learned to eat them. The roots were not as big and sweet then as they are now, but they must have tasted good enough to make the Indians want to grow them in their gardens and improve them.

When Columbus and other Spanish explorers discovered the sweet potato, they sent it back home to Spain. With it went the Indian name *batata,* which soon changed to *potato.* Later its name was mixed up with that of another kind of potato, which is white and not sweet at all. In fact, the white potato is not even a root.

The Stems We Eat

3

America gave the world white potatoes as well as sweet potatoes, but we did not find this out for a long time. For years and years we have called our white potatoes Irish potatoes, even though they did not originally come from Ireland. Now we know more about their origin.

Many, many centuries ago Indian tribes living along the western coast of South America learned to use potatoes as food. The Incas of Peru were growing and eating potatoes two thousand years before Columbus discovered America. In fact, they grew many different kinds of them. The skins of their potatoes varied from white to pink, red, and purple; the potato itself was sometimes white, sometimes yellow, pink, or purple. Some were tiny and wrinkled; others were giant potatoes with a smooth skin. Many of these different kinds of potatoes are still found in the markets of Peru today.

The Spaniards who discovered western South America were much more interested in the gold and silver and precious stones they found in this new country than in potatoes, but they soon learned that potatoes were good food for the crews on their sailing ships. Probably potatoes were carried to

Spain in the early sixteenth century by the Spanish ships coming from the New World.

Peruvian pottery vessel in the shape of a potato, from approximately A.D. 300–450

Other explorers and travelers in the newly discovered lands of America also carried potatoes back to Europe. Sir Walter Raleigh is supposed to have introduced potatoes to England and Ireland. There is a story that Sir Walter gave potatoes to his gardener to plant on his Irish estate. When only tiny little fruits formed on the plants, the gardener became angry. "Is this the fine fruit from America you prize so highly?" he asked his master. Sir Walter Raleigh was disappointed too and told the gardener to dig up the weeds and throw them away. The gardener obeyed and while digging out the "weeds" found a bushel of potatoes! Whether or not this particular story is true, potatoes became very popular in Ireland. They soon became a main food crop, and potatoes were eaten for breakfast, dinner, and supper.

Other countries of Europe did not accept the potato so readily. Frederick the Great of Prussia encouraged the growing of potatoes in his country. He issued instructions on how to plant and grow them, and soon potatoes were widely used there. But in France people believed that potatoes were poisonous, and they did not get over this idea for a long time.

Gradually potatoes were accepted in all the countries of Europe. They were used very little in the United States until the Irish immigrants brought them here from Ireland. That is why we called them Irish potatoes, as many people still do today. But the potato is really an American plant that traveled from South America to Europe and then came back to this country from Ireland.

The potatoes that were first brought here were not nearly as good as the ones we eat today. Our potatoes are bigger, and the flesh is firmer.

potato eye

potato buds starting to grow

If you hold a potato in your hand and look at it carefully, you will find that there are eyes all over it. They are the places where buds will grow, and you can see by looking at them why they are called "eyes." Notice that there are more eyes at one end of the potato. At the exact opposite end, you will see a little round scar where the potato was attached to the underground stem. The potato itself is just the swollen end of this underground stem.

Everybody who has used potatoes knows that if you keep them in a bag in a moist, dark place they will begin to sprout. Green stems will grow out of the eyes of the potato. Farmers use this knowledge when planting their potato crops. Sometimes they plant small whole potatoes, known as seed potatoes, but often they cut potatoes into pieces, making sure there are two or three eyes on each piece, and plant them. New potato plants will grow from the eyes in these pieces.

Every piece of potato you plant must have an eye on it in order to grow. Prove it with this experiment. Cut a potato into several pieces, so there are two or three eyes on at least one piece and no eyes at all on another. Let the cut ends of the potato dry. Then plant each piece three inches deep in a large flowerpot, using one pot for each piece. Use sterile potting soil that can be bought in any seed store or at a five-and-ten. Keep the soil in each pot moist but not wet. Within a short time, the piece of potato with eyes on it will sprout stems and leaves. Nothing will grow from the piece with no eye on it.

As the plant grows, interesting things are happening underground. Underground stems, or stolons, grow out from the plant, creeping sideways through the earth. Usually the

potato plant aboveground

stolons stay underground, but if one of them pokes through the earth into the light, it becomes a green, leafy stem.

When the stems of the potato plant are about six inches high (allow two weeks' growing time), you can see the underground stolons yourself if you take the plant out of the pot. Knock it out by turning the pot upside down and rapping the rim against something hard till the ball of earth in the pot comes out in one piece. Then carefully wash off the underground parts so you can see what has happened. You can tell the stolons from the roots, because they are thick, long shoots. The roots are thin and branched.

As the potato plant grows, the green leaves manufacture more food than the plant can use. The extra food passes down to the underground stolons, and slowly but surely little knobs form at the ends of the stolons. The knobs get bigger and bigger until they are full-sized potatoes.

You won't be able to see this happen in a flowerpot. But if you can possibly do so, plant some pieces of potatoes with eyes on them in the open ground of a garden. Wait until one of the plants blossoms and dig it up carefully. Tiny potatoes will be forming at the ends of the stolons. When the potatoes are big enough to be harvested, you can

potato plant belowground

STOLON

POTATO FORMING

potato plant in flower

see the little round scar on each one where it was attached to the underground stolon.

Many potato plants produce flowers, but few of them produce seed from the flowers. When the flowers do turn into fruit, the fruits are small, green, and inedible. The seeds are inside them. But nobody grows potatoes from seed. It is much easier, faster, and surer to grow new plants from cut pieces of potatoes or from whole, small seed potatoes.

Farmers all over the world plant their potato fields this way. The easy method has helped to make potatoes the most important vegetable in the world.

We also eat many stems that grow above the ground, the way most stems do. The tender young fleshy stems of asparagus are a good example. This plant needs three years to grow the delicious shoots we eat each spring.

Soon after you plant an asparagus seed, thin little stems will appear above the ground. They are not good to eat and grow out into green feathery tops. At the same time, a flat

asparagus plant

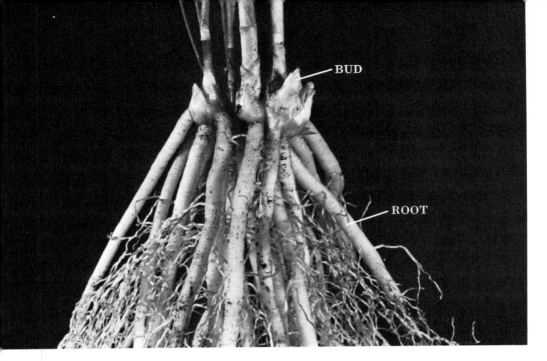

BUD

ROOT

crown of an asparagus plant

piece of underground stem with buds and a small clump of fleshy roots develop under the ground. The roots and buds are called the "crown" of the asparagus plant. When winter comes the tops die, but the plant is not dead. Under the ground there is still life. In the spring new shoots grow from the underground stem, and new fleshy roots form. The underground clump is getting big now, but the plant is still not ready to eat. Again the young shoots grow out into feathery tops.

We wait impatiently for the third year of the plant's life, for in the spring of this year the plant sprouts the thick, fleshy shoots, called "spears," we like to eat. From this time on, and for another fifteen to twenty years, we have no more work to do on the asparagus bed except to fertilize it. The plants are perennials; they stay alive from year to year.

Each spring new shoots come up from the underground parts. From March until June, when the spears are nine to ten inches long, we cut them off and eat them. Then the shoots become thinner. We stop cutting them and allow the stems to grow out into tall, feathery green tops. All summer long the green tops of the asparagus plants manufacture food in the sunlight. As in the case of the potato, more food is made than the plant uses, and the extra food is stored below in the root clump, which keeps on getting bigger.

asparagus spears

Most people do not plant asparagus seed. They buy and plant one-year-old crowns so that they do not have to wait too long for a crop.

There are two different kinds of asparagus plants. One bears only female flowers. The other has only male flowers.

asparagus flowers

asparagus fruits

The pollen from the male flowers is carried to the female flowers by insects. The male flowers drop off, but the female flowers develop into the little red berries that dot the asparagus plant. Inside the red berries are black seeds.

Billions of wild asparagus plants still grow along the seashore and riverbanks of southern Europe and Asia Minor.

asparagus seed in the fruit

Horses and cattle graze on this wild asparagus, and some people still gather it. Long ago the Greeks gathered it. The Romans also gathered it, but they cultivated it in their gardens, too. Gradually the use of asparagus spread to other countries.

Though asparagus has been known and grown for two thousand years, there is very little difference between the improved plant and the wild asparagus. Other plants have changed so much in cultivation that you can hardly see the connection between them and their wild ancestors, but asparagus has remained pretty much the same.

The Leaves We Eat

4

We all know what leaves look like. They grow out of the stem of a plant, and they have two parts: a stalk and a flat, broad part known as the leaf blade. Sometimes we eat a little bit of the stem with the leaves, as in the case of watercress. Sometime we eat just the leaf blades, as in the case of lettuce. Sometimes, when it is very big and thick, we eat only the stalk of the leaf as in the case of celery and rhubarb. Sometimes the leaves are fleshy and wrapped together in what we call a "bulb," like the onion. We eat leaves all the time.

People have been eating leafy plants for thousands of years. Persian kings ate lettuce in 550 B.C. The Greek philosopher Aristotle praised it more than two thousand years ago. And the Romans loved lettuce. They also liked parsley. It is said that in ancient Rome not a sauce or a salad was served without it.

Swiss chard is another leafy plant eaten in ancient times. It is a close relative of the beet and, like it, developed from the sea beet that grows along the Mediterranean Sea. For thousands of years the leaves of chard have been picked and cooked as greens.

celery stalks and leaves

Wild celery, the ancestor of our celery, also grows along the Mediterranean. It has no tall, thick leaf stalks, and its leaves are tough and bitter. The Romans used this plant for flavoring and as a medicine, but it wasn't eaten until hundreds of years later. In the seventeenth century somebody wrote that wild celery became milder and less "ungrateful" when it was cultivated. Afterward the plant was improved steadily until it had developed long fleshy stalks. Evidently it still had an unpleasantly strong flavor; for a long time the stalks were kept white and mild-flavored by blanching them —hilling up soil around the growing stalks so that no light could reach them. We still use blanched celery today, although many people are shifting to unblanched, green celery, which is much richer in vitamins.

celery going to seed

Rhubarb is an ancient plant too, but it is difficult to trace its history, because there are several different kinds. Here is one story about how rhubarb got its name. Many centuries ago camel caravans laden with treasures and rhubarb root from the Far East halted at the River Rha, which is now the Volga. From there boats took their cargoes to Greece and Rome. Since the river was called Rha, and the plant had come from the so-called barbarous lands of the East, the Romans gave it the name *rha barbum*, which later became the word *rhubarb*. Perhaps this explanation is not true, but it *is* true that one kind of rhubarb has been used by the Chinese for centuries as a medicine. The Chinese rhubarb is bigger and coarser than the rhubarb we know. The medicine is prepared from the underground roots. They are dug up in the fall, peeled, cut into pieces, and dried. Rhubarb is a perennial, like asparagus. It comes up year after year from its underground parts. The parts above the ground consist of fleshy leafstalks and pale green leaf blades at the top. We eat *only the stalks*. The leaf blades are poisonous.

rhubarb leaf

LEAF BLADE

STALK OF LEAF

spinach   onion bulb

Spinach too was carried to the rest of the world from an Asian country—Persia—about fifteen hundred years ago.

Some of the oldest leaves we know are the fleshy ones of onion or garlic. An old inscription on the Great Pyramid in Egypt tells how much was spent for onions and garlic eaten by the laborers who built it almost four thousand years ago! Garlic has also been used since ancient times as a remedy for many diseases and as a charm against the evil eye and vampires. So far there is no real proof that it cures anything, and, of course, it does not work as a charm.

One of the best ways to learn about our leafy food plants is to grow a few of them yourself indoors. Fill plastic or clay flowerpots or any shallow plastic container with sterile potting soil to within an inch from the top. Plant lettuce seed of a leafy, or nonheading, kind of lettuce. Cover the lettuce seeds with a very light layer of soil, and press it down firmly over the seeds.

Grand Rapids leaf lettuce

Water it with a bulb spray, and slip a plastic bag over the container. Then put the container in a sunny window. Keep the soil moist but not soaking wet. In a week, tiny lettuce plants should come up. When the leaves are about two inches tall, thin out the crowded plants by pulling the largest ones and using them for salad. Lettuce is ready to eat when it forms its cluster of leaves. Later in the season, the stems grow out and become packed with tiny yellow flowers; then the leaves turn tough and bitter. Be sure to let a few of the lettuce plants grow to this later stage so you can see the flowers.

Plant garden cress, or pepper grass in the same way. Keep this container in a light but not sunny window. You

lettuce plant flowering   lettuce flowers

will be amazed at the speed with which this plant grows. Within three days it pops out of the ground, and in two or three weeks you can use the leaves. Cut them off one inch above the ground. New leaves will grow out from the bottom part of the plant, and you will be able to clip them again in a short time. The leaves are spicy and are good with cottage cheese or a salad.

The Leaves We Eat | 55

Plant mustard seeds. Scatter a tablespoon of them on the surface of the soil in a shallow container. Cover the seeds with a light dusting of soil. Then slip a plastic bag over the container. Put the container in a sunny window. The seeds germinate rapidly. When the seedlings are a few inches high, remove the bag. The tender young leaves can be harvested in four days. You can use them as a garnish for stews, salads, and soups, for they have a sharp, tangy taste.

mustard

Look at the spice and herb shelves in your supermarket or grocery for other seeds such as celery, dill, parsley, and coriander. Plant them the same way you planted lettuce, cress, and mustard seeds. All grow into plants with tasty leaves.

dill

parsley

You can also sprout onions from seed, or you can buy onion sets—really just small onions—and plant them in a container. The long, green, hollow leaves of young onions can be chopped and used wherever onion flavor is desired.

If you'd like to grow your own garlic, just break up a head of it into its separate cloves and plant each one. Each clove is a bulb in itself. (Remember, a bulb is a shortened stem surrounded by thick, fleshy leaves.) You can grow a whole new head of garlic from each clove.

Your collection of leafy plants will be good to eat, but don't forget to watch the way in which each of them grows. Always allow a few of them to go on growing so you can see their flowers and seeds. Spinach, lettuce, mustard, and cress are annuals; they flower in one season. Parsley, Swiss chard, and onions are biennials that take two years to bloom and produce seed. Rhubarb is a perennial.

The tea we drink comes from leaves too. In the wild, the tea tree grows to about thirty feet, but it is usually cut back to the size of a bush three to five feet tall so that it can be picked more easily. Pickers nip off the bud and the first two to four leaves from the young shoots and gather the rest. Four to five pounds of fresh leaves go to make one pound of tea ready for the teapot.

The tea plant is a relative of the camelia, but its flowers are much smaller and not as pretty. It is native to India from where it spread to China. At least we know that it was used in China twelve hundred years ago.

There is still another group of plants whose leaves we eat that deserves special attention. It is the cabbage tribe, whose ancestor can be found today growing wild along the seacoast of southern and western Europe. You would never

tea leaves

guess from looking at the wild cabbage weed that it is the ancestor of cabbage, kale, collards, Brussels sprouts, broccoli, and cauliflower. Many, many hundreds of years ago people gradually changed the wild cabbage into several different kinds of plants.

Some people preferred a vegetable with one big head. They kept picking out and saving the seeds of the wild cabbage plants that formed the best heads. This process of

cabbage head

selection century after century finally produced the cabbage plant we know today. In this plant there is practically no space on the stem between the leaves, and the leaves are gathered into one big head. Cut a cabbage in half down its length, and you will see the leaves coming out of the short stem in a beautiful pattern.

cross section of cabbage head

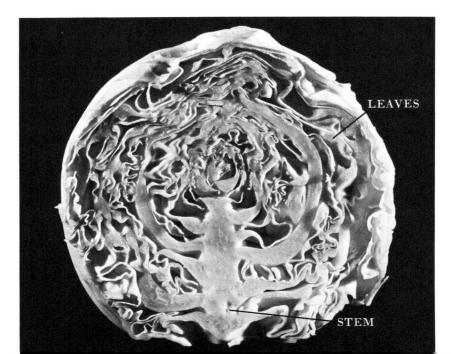

LEAVES

STEM

Other people may have preferred tiny little heads of leaves instead of one big cabbage head. They selected plants that tended to form little buds of leaves along the stem, and eventually they produced Brussels sprouts. This plant is sometimes known as the thousand-headed cabbage, because it has so many little miniature cabbageheads, but the more familiar name comes from the fact that it was first grown and developed around the town of Brussels in Belgium.

Brussels sprouts

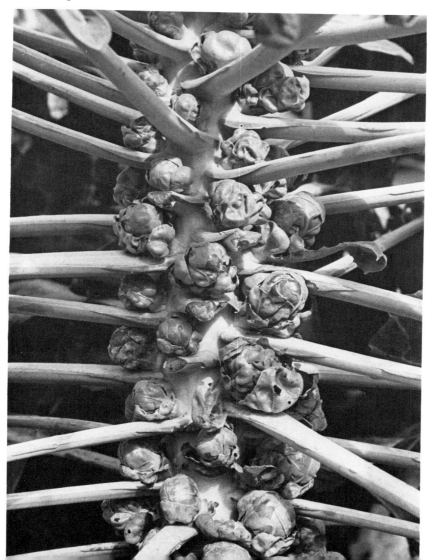

collard

Still other people preferred the loose, leafy types of wild cabbage. They gradually developed kale and collards. The leaves of kale are usually crimped and curled; collard leaves are smooth and large and soft. Both of these plants are very rich in minerals and vitamins. Dutch people sometimes say that their childrens' red cheeks come from the large amount of kale they get with their meals!

Broccoli and cauliflower also developed from the wild cabbage plant, but we eat the flower stalks and flower buds, not the leaves, of these plants.

Experiments done in England have helped to prove that the wild cabbage was the real ancestor of this whole cabbage tribe. Wild cabbage was gathered from rocks overhanging the sea in Wales. The plants were grown in gardens, and seeds of those plants that looked different from the others were saved and replanted. Finally plants that resembled broccoli and cabbage and kale were developed.

When you look at cabbage, kale, collards, Brussels sprouts, broccoli, and cauliflower in the vegetable store, it is hard to realize that they are related. But you can see for yourself that there is a connection between them. Empty a package of cabbage seed into a dish, and you will notice that the seeds are round and brownish. Empty packages of the kale, collards, Brussels sprouts, broccoli, and cauliflower

seeds of cauliflower and cabbage

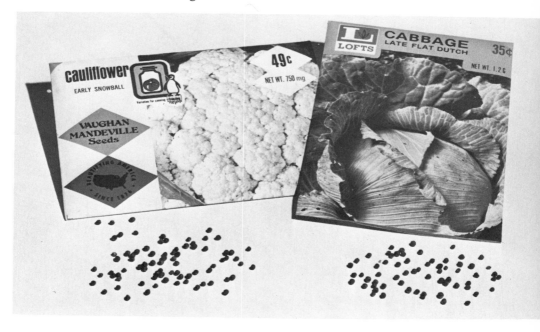

into the same dish. You will not be able to tell them apart. The seeds of every one of them are round and brownish.

If you plant these seeds you will discover another interesting thing. Put a few seeds of each one of these vegetables into separate flowerpots containing sterile potting soil, and cover them with a half inch of it. Be sure to label them. If you do not, you won't be able to identify the young plants when they sprout. In this early stage of growth, they all look alike. As they grow, they begin to develop in their own special ways.

All of the cabbage tribe are biennials. They become the vegetables we know during their first year of growth. If they are left in the ground, a flower stalk comes up the following year. Since they all belong to one family, their flower stalks and flowers look very much the same.

The Flowers We Eat

5

When we think of flowers, we think of those we gather to make bouquets—the marigolds, petunias, roses, and carnations that we love because they are so pretty. It almost seems a joke to say we eat flowers. Yet some of the vegetables we eat—cauliflower, broccoli, and artichokes—are really flowers.

Cauliflower comes from the Latin words *caulis*, which means cabbage, and *floris*, meaning flower. Like the other members of the cabbage tribe, cauliflower developed from wild cabbage. But the thick, fleshy flower stalks of this plant are the parts that have become good to eat, rather than the leaves. When it sprouts from the seed, it looks like every other member of the cabbage family; but soon a green button develops in the center of the plant. This button is the beginning of the flower head. When it forms, the gardener gathers together the outside cabbagelike leaves and ties them over it to keep out the light. As the plant grows, the leaves get bigger and the green flower head inside them becomes large and white and thick. If the flower head were left uncovered, it would turn brown.

Cut a cauliflower head down the middle to see the short

flower head of cauliflower

cauliflower cross section

FLOWER BUDS

FLOWER STALK

fleshy flower stalks and the thick little clusters of buds at the top of them. If the flower head is not picked and the plant is protected from frost during the winter, it will grow ordinary flower stalks like those of other cabbage plants in the spring.

Broccoli is another vegetable whose flowers we eat. Like cauliflower, it is a descendant of the wild cabbage that developed into a plant with thick flower stalks. The stalk is longer, however, and the cluster of flower buds is not packed so tightly. Both the stalks and buds of broccoli are green, instead of white as they are in cauliflower.

broccoli

FLOWER BUDS

FLOWER STALK

One broccoli plant will produce food through a long season. After the first main flower heads are picked, new side shoots bearing flower buds appear.

Put some broccoli stalks in water for a few days, and the flower buds will open out into yellow flowers.

Broccoli has been popular in Italy for hundreds of years. It was brought to this country by Italians, who grew it here for many years before it became popular.

The artichoke is a flower bud too. Have you ever eaten one? If you have, you peeled off leaf after leaf and dipped each one into a sauce of butter, or French dressing, before eating the delicious fleshy part at the base of the leaf. Finally you came to the heart of the artichoke. Before you could eat it, though, you had to cut off the prickly choke on top of it.

You were eating a gigantic flower bud. The leaves are

artichoke flower bud and cross section

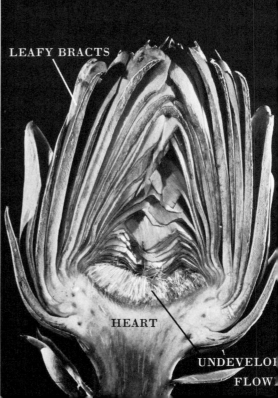

LEAFY BRACTS

HEART

UNDEVELOP
FLOW

not really leaves; they are the leaflike parts of the flower bud. The heart is the fleshy base from which the flowers grow. In fact, when you cut off the choke you cut off the undeveloped flowers.

Artichoke flower buds are picked off the growing plant before they open. If they are left on the plant they open up into gigantic heads of purple flowers that look like those of the thistle. There are thousands of tiny flowers on each big flower head. The green leaflike parts around the heart of the artichoke open out. By the time the flower blooms, they are hard and tough and no longer fit to eat.

Seeds develop at the bottom of the artichoke flower head after the flowers are pollinated. But artichokes are rarely grown from seed. They are perennial; the underground parts stay alive from year to year and send up new shoots each spring. The plant grows to a height of about four feet. Its silvery-gray, deeply cut leaves and purple flowers are so beautiful that in some places the plant is grown just for ornament.

The big purple flower heads that look so much like the wild thistle give you a clue to the artichoke's history. Its ancestor was a thistle plant with the name of cardoon. Two thousand years ago, in Rome, it was a favorite vegetable. People did not eat the flower buds then; they liked the young leaves and stalks, which were grown in the dark to make them white and tender. Our modern artichoke was developed somewhere in Italy from the cardoon plant. The use of artichokes as food spread from Italy to other countries of the world.

The Fruits We Eat | 6

You must look into the flower of a plant to find where the fruit will grow. Every fruit in the world comes from a part of the flower called the "ovary," which is located at the base of the pistil. The pistil always grows in the center of the flower, and it has three parts—the stigma, style, and ovary. Inside the ovary are ovules, or seeds-to-be.

Ovules can become seeds only if they are pollinated. Pollen forms in the anthers—little bags on the top of the stamens around the pistil of the flower. When it is ripe, the pollen becomes dry and dusty and usually sifts out of the anther through a slit or a little hole. Sometimes wind carries it to the stigma of the pistil. Sometimes insects carry it. When it lands on the stigma of the pistil, the pollen grain grows a tube down through the style to the ovules in the ovary. All the living matter in the pollen tube combines with the living matter in the ovule. Now the ovule is fertilized and can begin to change into a seed. At the same time, the ovary changes too. It grows bigger as the seeds develop, and finally it becomes the fruit. The scientific definition of a fruit is that part of the plant that has seeds in it.

A tomato is a fruit, but sixty years ago there was quite

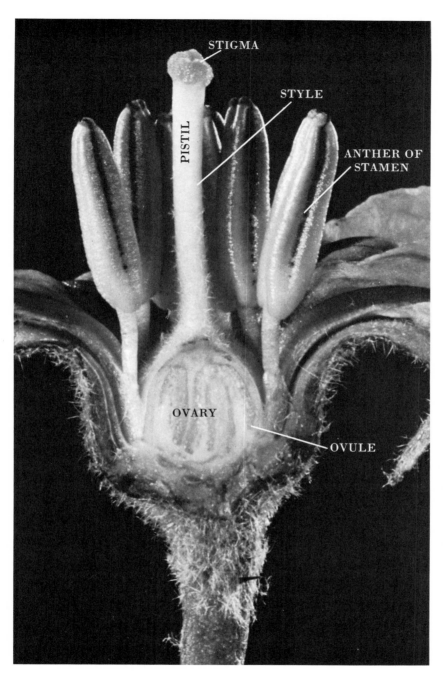

cross section of typical flower

tomatoes

an argument over whether the tomato was a fruit or a vegetable. Importers did not have to pay duty on fruit at that
time, but they did have to pay duty on vegetables. The
tomato importers took the case to court, where the judge
decided that the tomato was a vegetable, because it was
usually served at dinner with the main part of the meal. So
the tomato became legally a vegetable, although plant scien-

tists still know that it is a fruit. It has seeds in it, which develop from the ovary of the tomato flower.

The tomato ovary grows bigger and bigger after pollination. The petals and all other flower parts fall off as the little round green ball grows to its full size. Then the color changes from green to red, and the tomato is ready to be plucked from the plant and eaten.

At one time everybody in the United States thought tomatoes were poisonous. So people did not eat them, although they grew them in flower gardens and window boxes because their fruits were pretty.

The story is told that one day, in the year 1820, a man named Robert Gibbon Johnson carried a basket of tomatoes to the steps of the courthouse at Salem, New Jersey, and offered some to the people gathered there. Nobody would touch them. Mr. Johnson then calmly ate up the whole basketful. He did not fall down dead, as everyone had expected. In fact, he remained healthy and strong. He had been eating tomatoes for a long time, and he felt that other people should eat this delicious fruit too. The news of the incident spread quickly. It helped to make people accept the idea that tomatoes were good food.

It seems peculiar that the efforts of many people were needed to get the tomato accepted as a food plant in this country, when the Indians in Mexico had been growing tomatoes and eating them for hundreds of years before white men ever came to America. There are many wild and primitive kinds of tomatoes still growing today in the mountains around Peru. Peru was the tomato's native home, but Mexico is where it first became an important part of the national diet. And it was probably from Mexico that the tomato spread all around the world. Like the potato, the tomato went from America to Europe and then came back again to our own country.

ovary of the tomato flower

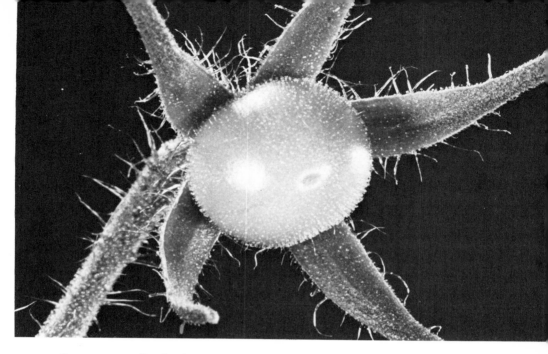

tomato flower ovary developing

The exact course of this journey is hard to trace, however. Some people say the plant was first carried to Spain and from there to North Africa, where it was grown in Moorish gardens long before it was carried to Italy. People who make this claim base it on word evidence. They say that is why the Italians called it *pomo dei Mori* (Moor's apple). But others say it was really called *pomo d'oro* (golden apple) in Italy, because the tomatoes first introduced there were yellow or golden.

In either case, the tomato was quickly accepted in Italy. The Italians were the first Europeans to eat it. They developed many new varieties and used them in preparing the wonderful tomato sauces that became such an important part of Italian cooking.

When the tomato spread to France, its Italian name was changed to *pomme d'amour*, which means love apple. And so in England the tomato became known as a love apple, and the people who first came to America brought this name with them. It lasted a long time. Your grandmother probably called the tomato a love apple.

Italian-Americans were probably chiefly responsible for getting tomatoes accepted as food in this country. They were accustomed to using them and so helped get rid of the notion that they were poisonous. Today tomatoes are the third leading truck crop and the most important canning crop in the United States.

A long time was needed for tomatoes to be accepted as a food plant, but peppers, which were also found here by the Spanish explorers, became popular right away. Both sweet and hot American peppers traveled all over the world and became immediately successful. In those days, when there were no refrigerators to keep food from spoiling, spices were treasured. They preserved food and helped to make spoiled food taste better. The discoverers of America were looking for a short route to the Orient and its spices when they landed in the West Indies. When Columbus found the Indians using a fiery, hot fruit, he thought it was a kind of pepper, like the black pepper spice of India. American peppers were really very different from the Indian black pepper spice, but the name *pepper* stuck. And because it could be used as a spice, the new pepper plant was quickly accepted all over the world.

The Indians of the West Indies were not the only ones growing peppers at the time America was discovered. The Indian peoples of Mexico, Peru, Chile, and other parts of the American tropics were growing every kind of pepper. We are still growing these different kinds of peppers today. We have tabasco pepper, from which we make tabasco sauce. We have chili peppers, which we use for chili seasoning. Cayenne pepper is the dried ground fruit of still another kind of pepper. One kind of pepper developed in Hungary gives us paprika. Another kind is the pimiento pepper, the heart-shaped, thick-fleshed red sweet pepper that is used to stuff olives or to trim salads. And there are, of course, our ordinary sweet green peppers that are used while they are still green, before they ripen into a red color. Tabasco, chili, and cayenne peppers are hot, peppery kinds that sting and burn your tongue. The pimiento and green garden peppers are sweet. But if you taste the seeds of the green pepper you will find the same hot sting in the seeds, although it is not in the fleshy part.

Like all other fruits, the pepper grows from the ovary

green pepper   tabasco pepper

of the flower. Pepper flowers open in the morning right after sunrise and are pollinated by insects.

Our pepper plants have no relation to the black pepper from which we get our table spice. Black pepper spice is the fruit of large vines that grow in the Orient. The fruit is ground up to give us the pepper we put on our tables, along with salt.

You can get really mixed up about the difference between a vegetable and a fruit if you don't stick to the scientific definition of a fruit: the part of the plant that contains seeds. Otherwise, you'd never recognize the fruit of some of our vine crops for what it is. The cucumber, for example, is the fruit of the cucumber vine, but everybody says the

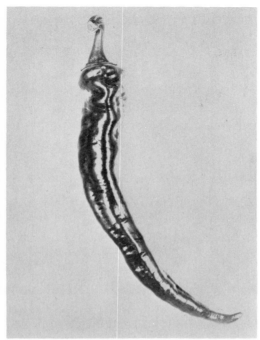

chili pepper   cayenne pepper

cucumber is a vegetable. We also say squashes and pumpkins are vegetables, although they are really fruits. On the
other hand, we don't have the same trouble about the fruit
of the watermelon and other melon vines. We are accustomed to thinking of them as fruits.

All of these vine crops—cucumbers, squashes, pumpkins, and melons—are closely related. They all belong to
the same family of plants, and they look a lot alike. They
all have large, deeply lobed leaves and big yellow flowers.
Most of them have two different kinds of flowers on the same
plant. One, the male flower, has only stamens in it; these
parts are joined together into a knob and produce pollen.
The other has only the pistil in it. The lower end of the

OVARY OF FEMALE
CUCUMBER FLOWER
DEVELOPING INTO
CUCUMBER

cucumber flower

pistil, the ovary, develops into the fruit of the vine. You see it as a little green bulge below the petals of the female flower. Bees transfer the pollen from the male flowers that produce it to the female flowers, and soon afterward the green ball begins to swell. The yellow petals above it wither and die, while the ovary below changes into a pumpkin, or a cucumber, or a squash, or a melon.

Collect the seeds of squash, cucumber, pumpkin, watermelon, and muskmelon. Notice that they vary a lot in size, but otherwise they look much alike. Just as in the case of the cabbage tribe, the seeds of these vine crops show that they all belong to one family.

All of these seeds have an interesting way of breaking out of the seed coats. The root that first grows out of the seed has a little peg on it that very neatly holds the two

PEG

squash seed sprouting

parts of the seed coat apart while the seed leaves are drawn out. Grow a few pumpkin or squash or melon seeds yourself to see this process. Line a tumbler with wet paper towels, and place the seeds between the glass and the towel. Leave an inch of water at the bottom of the glass. In this way, you will be able to see exactly how the root peg does its work.

Though cucumbers, squashes, pumpkins, and melons are so much alike in their way of growth, they come from many different countries of the world. Melons originally came from Persia. Cucumbers came from India. The native home of watermelons is Africa, where you can still find whole districts covered with wild watermelon plants. Squashes and pumpkins originated in America. When the first explorers came here, different kinds of pumpkins and squashes were growing throughout North and South America. In fact, the English word *squash* comes from the Indian word *askutasquash*.

All of the members of this family have been known since ancient times. No one is sure how wild squashes and pumpkins came to be used as food, because all the wild kinds are small and bitter. But the clue to the puzzle seems to be that they were first used as rattles in primitive ceremonies and dances. When the fruits of squash and pumpkins dry, the seeds rattle around inside as they do in the

string bean flowers

maraca, a musical instrument of modern bands. Perhaps as people grew and cultivated the fruits for their use as rattles, they changed from the small, bitter, wild kinds to the sweet, fleshy kinds we know today.

Bean and pea pods are also fruits. They grow from the ovary of the bean or pea flower and have seeds inside. Sometimes we eat just the beans or peas, shelled from the pods. And sometimes we eat the whole pod, with the seeds inside, as is the case with string, or snap, beans.

Peas and beans belong to the same family of plants,

pod forming from ovary of string bean flower

and their flowers look much the same. Both resemble small sweet-pea flowers. All of these flowers have a large banner petal, two wing petals, and two curved petals that are joined together. If you spread open the jointed front petals, you will find the pistil and stamens hidden inside. The pistil is long and looks like a tiny bean or pea pod. After pollination, which is usually by pollen from the same flowers, the ovary of the pistil swells into a ripe bean or pea pod. The seeds inside become peas or beans. Even though they are related, beans and peas have very different histories. Beans come from America; peas first grew in the Middle East.

Peas have been known for a very long time. They have even been found buried in lake mud established as five thousand years old. From somewhere in the middle of Asia, peas spread throughout the rest of the world. Greeks and Romans mentioned peas in their writings, but they didn't seem to like them very much. Peas did not become really popular until the end of the seventeenth century, when royal society in France went mad about them. Madame de Maintenon, one of the court ladies at that time, wrote: "The subject of peas continues to absorb all others. The anxiety to eat them, the pleasure of having eaten them, and the desire to eat them again are the three great matters which have been discussed by our princes for four days past. Some ladies, even after having supped at the royal table, and well supped too, upon returning to their own homes, at the risk of suffering from indigestion, will again eat peas before going to bed. It is both a fashion and a madness."

Now peas are no longer a "madness," but they are very popular in our own country. Peas are the next largest canning crop after tomatoes.

A long time passed before peas traveled to this country from Asia, but beans were being grown here for many hundreds of years before explorers discovered this continent. In Europe and Asia, only a few kinds of beans were known. Here in America explorers found hundreds of different kinds of beans being used as food by the Indians. There were lima beans, kidney beans, white navy beans, black beans, pinto beans, string beans, wax beans, and many other kinds being grown all over North, South, and Central America. Practically every tribe grew a different kind of bean and had a different name for it. They were important to the Indians because they are rich in protein, just as meat is. For the tribes that used little or no meat, beans helped to provide an adequate diet.

Another native American plant used by the Indians is the peanut. The peanut belongs in the same family as peas and beans. Like them, it is rich in protein, and it also has lots of oil.

Peanuts were popular with the Indian people of America for hundreds of years before the arrival of Columbus. We know this fact because many mummies found in Peru in tombs more than fifteen hundred years old were buried with a grave offering of peanuts. Many tombs also contained jars with peanut designs. Merchants carried peanuts from South America to Africa and across the Pacific to China. In both countries, the peanut grew so well and spread so widely that after a while the people in Africa and China thought it had been growing there forever! But we know now that peanuts went from South America to all parts of the world.

Since peanuts belong in the same family as beans and

Peruvian jar more than 1500 years old

peas, you can guess that the flowers of the peanut plant look like pea and bean flowers. The whole plant in blossom looks like a pea vine with yellow flowers, but peanut flowers do not behave like ordinary flowers at all. Instead of changing into fruit right where it is, each flower, after it is pollinated, starts growing down toward the ground. The petals fall off, and the ovary begins to develop into a fruit; but the fruit will not ripen unless it pushes down into the earth. That is why you have to dig for peanuts, even though they are fruits!

peanuts forming underground

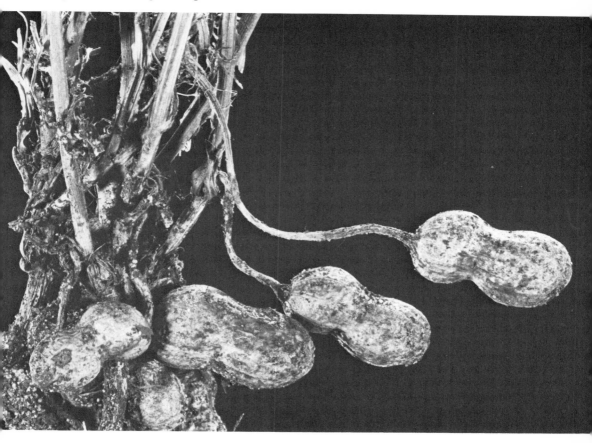

Apples, pears, peaches, plums, and cherries—most of the fruits we think of as fruit—came from faraway places. Some of them were known and grown for thousands of years before they were brought to this country. Apples, pears, cherries, grapes, and some plums originated, for example, somewhere in southwestern Asia. They had spread all over Europe by the time America was discovered. Peaches, apricots, and different kinds of plums were carried from their native home in China to the Mediterranean countries more than two thousand years ago. They, too, were being eaten all over Europe before the discovery of the New World.

The first Europeans who came to America to live brought seeds of these fruits with them. Thousands and thousands of young apple trees were planted and grown from apple seeds brought here by the early settlers. In the early 1800's, Johnny Appleseed traveled through the wilderness from Pennsylvania to Illinois planting apple seeds wherever he could. He gave apple seeds to any settler he met who promised to take care of the young trees that grew from them.

Unfortunately, people were often disappointed when their young trees started to bear fruit. They discovered that an apple tree grown from seed may not produce the same kind of apple as the parent tree. This variation was quite different from what happened with good vegetable seeds. If, for instance, you plant lettuce seed from a particularly good kind of lettuce plant, you will usually grow a lettuce crop very much like the parent plant from which the seeds came. In the case of apples and other fruits, this principle didn't seem to work. Seeds of a very fine apple, pear, peach, or apricot tree might or might not produce as good

apples

fruit as its parent. Usually the fruit was not as good, but sometimes it was much better. Some wonderful new varieties were discovered among the thousands of apple trees that were planted from seed in this country.

One day a Canadian farmer named John McIntosh found a delicious new kind of apple growing on one of the wild apple trees near his orchards. It has become known as the McIntosh apple. The Baldwin apple was discovered in 1793 near Lowell, Massachusetts, by a surveyor working on a canal. Many other good varieties had been discovered before this time. Many of the new American varieties soon became even better than their ancestors from Europe!

New varieties would not have improved the quality of the apples, however, if they had had to be replanted from seed. Fortunately, there was another way of growing more trees without planting seeds. It had been used in Europe

golden delicious apple branch grafted onto the stub of a young apple tree

for a long time and was called "grafting." A branch of one tree whose apples were good was cut off and joined to the stem of another tree whose roots were well-grown. The two parts were tied together tightly until they actually grew together; then the other branches of the tree with good roots were cut off. From that time on, the tree produced apples only from the branch that was grafted to it. In this way, people could grow a new apple tree much faster than if they planted seeds, and they were sure of getting the kind of apples they wanted.

Grafting made it possible to grow thousands of trees from any new variety. McIntosh apple trees soon spread all over the country, because people bought branches of those trees for grafting to other, poorer apple trees.

Pears, plums, peaches, and apricots were all improved in the same way. The accidental discovery of superior trees among thousands of seedling trees came first. Then these trees were multiplied by grafting. Sometimes the best types were found in Europe, sometimes in Asia, sometimes in America. Sometimes different types of trees were carefully cross-pollinated (the pollen from one put onto the stigmas of the other) so new kinds of trees grew from their seeds. Always, the new varieties were increased by grafting.

Apples, pears, cherries, plums, peaches, and apricots all belong to the rose family of plants. They do not resemble each other very much in shape or size or the way they branch, but their flowers reveal their family connection.

The ovaries of these flowers become fruit in different ways. In the case of apples and pears, the flower parts around the ovary and the ovary itself form the fruit. Most of the fleshy part of the apple or pear comes from these flower parts around the ovary; only the core of the fruit comes from the ovary alone.

In the case of plums, cherries, peaches, and apricots, only the ovary becomes the fleshy fruit. The inner wall of the ovary becomes hard and stony. When you take out the pit

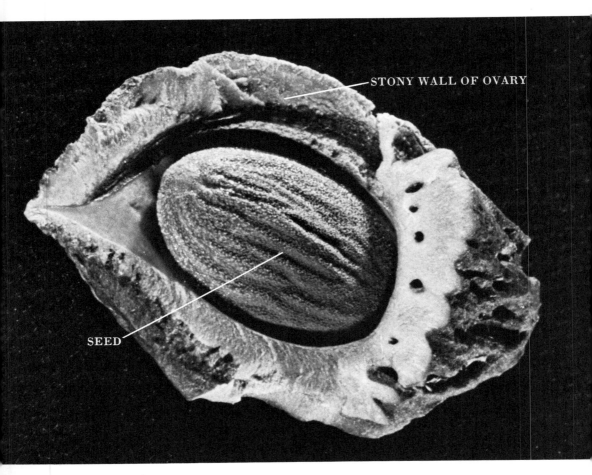

STONY WALL OF OVARY

SEED

peach pit

of a plum, a cherry, a peach, or an apricot, you are holding a stony wall of the ovary. You have to crack it open to see the seed inside. Do so, and find the real seeds inside the pits of these fruits.

Strawberries, raspberries, and blackberries were growing wild in America when this country was discovered. One colonist wrote home to England that she stepped on strawberries wherever she put her foot down! And many a colonist tore his shirt on the thorns of the wild raspberry and blackberry bushes! But America was not the only place where these fruits were growing. They were found all over the world at this time. They, too, belong to the rose family and have flowers that strongly resemble those of apple, pear, peach, and plum.

The pineapple is another native American fruit. Columbus saw it when he landed in the West Indies at the end of his second voyage in 1493. The Indians used pineapple juice as a medicine taken internally to reduce fever. They also used the juice externally to cure skin sores. Besides eating the fruit, they cooked pineapple with meat to make

strawberries

it more tender. It was a luscious fruit and quickly spread throughout the world.

People who have been in the tropics say that you do not know what a pineapple can taste like until you have eaten one that has ripened on the plant. The reason is that most of the sugar goes into the fruit from the stem in the very last stage of ripening. The pineapples you buy in the store have been taken from the plant while still unripe, and so they lack the sweetness of this final ripening.

What does a pineapple plant look like? You can get a good idea of it if you look at the crown of leaves that comes out of the top of the pineapple and imagine it about six times larger than it is. The leaves are stiff and large and spiny. In the second year of its growth, a giant cone-shaped flower cluster forms at the top of the plant. The purplish-blue flowers open on this cluster from the bottom up. For about twenty days, new flowers keep opening each day. As the flowers are pollinated and the petals fall, the ovary of each flower becomes a little fruit that is joined to the ones next to it and to the core in the center to make one great, big pineapple. In this plant, the whole flower cluster made up of many flowers joins together to form a fruit—which is really a cluster of fruits. You can see the separate fruits if you look at a pineapple.

The pineapple plant is a perennial, but after four or five years the fruit becomes smaller and smaller. For this reason, commercial growers replant their fields every few years or so, using suckers, or shoots, from the old plants for rooting.

pineapple plant

banana cutters at work

Another delicious tropical fruit is the banana. The banana is not native to the American tropics, like the pineapple; it grows very well there, but its first home was the humid tropical jungles of southern Asia. When south-Asiatic people traveled eastward over the islands of the Pacific, they carried the banana with them. It also went with travelers going in the opposite direction, across the Indian Ocean to Africa. From there it went to the Canary Islands, off the west coast of Africa, and then across the Atlantic to the West Indies and America. By the time it reached America it had circled the globe, for there it met bananas that had come the opposite way, from the Philippine Islands.

A banana "tree" certainly looks like a tree—it grows to a height of fifteen to thirty feet—but it is not, because it does not have a true stem above the ground. The real stem of the banana plant is under the ground. Like the potato, the stem has buds, or eyes, on it. When pieces of this underground stem, each with at least one eye, are planted, huge leaves appear above the ground within three or four weeks. The base of these leaves, rolled tightly together, look like the trunk, or stem, of the banana "tree."

You can make a paper model of a banana tree from a piece of standard typewriter paper, 8½ by 11 inches in size. Fold it in half, then fold it again so that you have four equal sections. Cut the sections apart and shape them, as shown in the drawings, into four banana leaves. Now roll each leaf around a pencil, and fasten the roll with scotch tape. Each leaf roll should be a little narrower than the one before. Fit one leaf into the other. Roll the free ends over a pencil so they wave gently backward, and you have

paper model of banana tree

a paper model of the banana tree. You can see clearly that the banana trunk is the joined-together bases of leaves, rather than a real stem. Each leaf of the banana plant is huge, big enough to provide a quick umbrella for anyone caught in a tropical downpour.

About a year after planting, a huge flower stalk pushes up from the underground stem of the banana plant through the hollow trunk and unfurls in the center of the crown of leaves. The flowers are in clusters, each cluster framed by a brilliant red sheath. Each cluster of flowers develops into a cluster of bananas. This plant is unusual in that no pollen is necessary to fertilize the ovaries. They develop into bananas without it. As the ovaries ripen, they turn upward. When we see bananas in the store, the fruit is usually turned upside down.

Bananas are still green when they are harvested. Unlike the pineapple, they lose their flavor if left to ripen on the plant. Each plant bears one bunch of bananas. Then the tree is cut down close to the ground, where it quickly rots and becomes good fertilizer. New plants are always coming up from the underground stem; when one plant is cut down, there are others growing up to replace it. Once a banana field is planted, it produces bananas for years and years.

The bananas we eat have no real seeds in them. The little brown specks are just ghosts of seeds, and the whole fruit is soft and pulpy. But there are several kinds of bananas that are quite different. They have no pulp at all, just an outer shell containing large seeds, which fill the shell as peas fill a pea pod. Other kinds have more pulp. Scientists think that as people used bananas they kept picking out the plants that had pulpy fruit. They took good care of the shoots that came out of the underground stems of these plants. By continually saving and planting shoots that bore bananas with lots of pulp and very few seeds, we finally developed our seedless banana of today.

One of the very interesting things about a banana plant is the speed with which it grows. Three months after the rootstock is planted, the banana plant is three feet high. In six months it is ten feet high. (If it were in your house it would reach the ceiling.) At nine months it has reached its full height of twenty to thirty feet!

Oranges and lemons and limes can be traced back to their native homes in the warmer parts of Southeast Asia. They, too, had spread from Asia to all of Europe before they were brought to this country. Sour oranges were introduced into Florida by the Spaniards, and Indian tribes spread them around all the lakes and rivers of the state. But if you ever find an orange tree growing outside of a regular grove of trees in Florida, don't taste the fruit. Its sour taste will pucker your mouth.

Sweet oranges come from another kind of orange tree. When this tree was introduced here, the sour orange trees already planted were used as grafting stock. Branches of sweet oranges were grafted onto hardy sour orange trees that already had good root systems, so less time was needed to develop groves of sweet orange trees.

Do you know what the navel orange is like—with its thick skin, meaty pulp, and a little bump at one end? All navel oranges in the United States can be traced to two trees that were sent from Brazil to Riverside, California, in 1873. From these two trees, nine million navel orange trees were produced by grafting in California alone!

orange blossoms and fruit

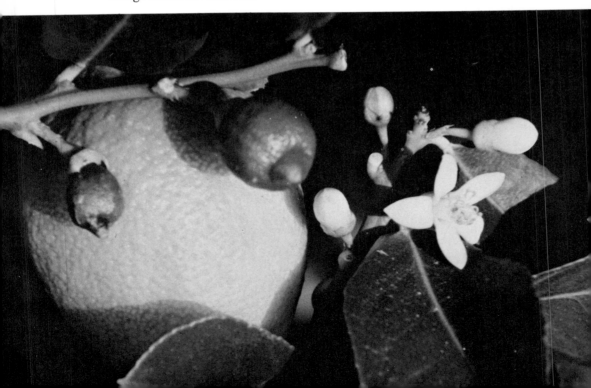

All oranges trees, as well as lemon and lime trees, grow only in regions where it does not get freezing cold in the winter. The trees stay green the year round. Their flowers are white and sweet-smelling. All resemble each other, for oranges, lemons, and limes are in the same family. Their fruits are much alike too. All have an outer rind that comes from the outer ovary wall and a juicy pulpy part that comes from the inside ovary walls.

If you ever see walnuts growing on trees, you may think they are young, unripe oranges. The walnut we know grows

English walnuts

inside a green, round husk. The whole green ball, including the walnut, is the fruit. The shell of the walnut, like the shell of the almond, is the hard inside wall of the ovary.

The English walnuts we eat really should be called Persian or Iranian walnuts, for that is where they came from. Black walnut trees growing in forests of the United States have nuts that are good to eat too, but, unlike that of the English walnut, the green husk does not crack open when the nut is ripe. The nuts have to be beaten out of the husk.

Brazil nuts grow on majestic trees in the Amazon jungles of Brazil. People who walk through these forests have to be careful that a great fruit of the Brazil nut tree does not drop onto their heads! Each one of these fruits weighs about three pounds. It has to be broken open by force to get at the dozen or so Brazil nuts, or seeds, that are inside. Chestnut burs are more obliging. These spiny coverings open and allow the chestnut fruits to fall out.

black walnut fruit

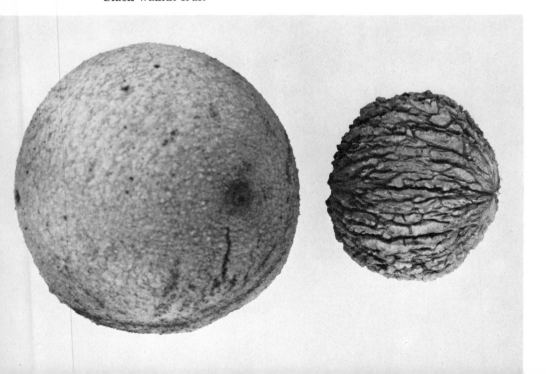

coconut cultivation in Indonesia

The coconut, another tropical fruit, can also be painful if it hits a person on the head when it falls from the tree. The coconuts are the fruits of the coconut palm, a tall, graceful tree that grows on many sandy shores of tropical islands. The coconuts hang in clusters at the top of the tree. When the coconuts fall, the tides carry them into the water. There they float because the husks around the seed are light. Inside the husk there is a tough waterproof shell. Because of its buoyancy and because of its waterproof shell, the coconut has been carried by ocean currents all around the world.

In the tropics, the coconut palm leaves are used for thatching houses. The fibers of the leaf are used to make ropes, mats, and clothes. The seeds are used as drinking vessels. The white flesh is a good food, and the liquid in the shell makes a sweet palm milk. Oil pressed from the seeds is used in margarine, in soaps and shampoos, and as a cooking oil. This tree is one of the most useful in the world.

Dates, olives, and figs are other fruits that are a basic part of the diet of some people. They have been known since ancient times.

The date tree is probably one of the oldest cultivated trees. Instructions for growing it were recorded five thousand years ago in Mesopotamia, now Iraq. It was considered the "tree of life" in the desert, for it provided food, mats, rope, and baskets. If you've ever seen a picture of an oasis in a desert, the trees there were probably date palm trees. These majestic palms grow in dry places where other trees cannot grow. Their roots must reach water, however, and for this reason, groves of date palm trees mark oases in the desert. Some date trees bear only female flowers, others only male flowers. The male flowers produce pollen, and only a few are allowed to grow for this purpose. The giant clusters of female flowers, sometimes ten thousand flowers to a cluster, are what become dates. We eat the sweet flesh of the fruit around the seed.

date palm tree

Olive trees are small. They have grayish-green leaves that stay on the tree throughout the year. Tiny little flowers ripen into the olive fruits we know. If the olives are picked while they are still unripe and green, we have green olives. Black olives are allowed to ripen on the tree until they are hard ripe. Olives grown for the oil in them ripen on the tree until they are soft ripe, so the oil can be more easily pressed out of them. If you ever pick an olive from a tree and taste it, you will wonder how men came to eat them.

fig tree

They are the bitterest things you can imagine. They have to be soaked in a lye solution before they get the flavor we like. It would be interesting to know how people first discovered that lye takes the bitter taste out of olives and that the olives taste even better if, after washing them to remove the lye, they are soaked in a strong salt solution.

The fruit of the fig tree is most unusual. The flowers are hidden away in a fleshy green ball with a hole on top. This green ball becomes a fig fruit. But it won't ripen unless a certain tiny wasp, which hatches in the male flowers of the wild fig, crawls into it to pollinate the little flowers inside. Smyrna figs were introduced into California a century ago, but they didn't bear fruit until 1899, when the special wasps were imported and allowed to grow in wild figs planted near the Smyrna figs.

The cocoa and coffee we drink are made from fruits. People who have seen the cocoa, or cacao, tree in fruit say it is an unforgettable sight. Big colored fruits like melons hang from the trunk and branches of the tree. If you took a quick look at a cocoa tree plantation, you might think the trees were hung with Chinese lanterns. Inside each huge fruit is a white, sticky pulp in which twenty to fifty almond-shaped seeds, or cacao beans, can be found. The seeds have to be separated from the pulp and dried before we use them to make cocoa or chocolate. Our word *chocolate* comes directly from the old Aztec word *chocolatl*. It is said that the Aztec Emperor Montezuma would drink nothing but chocolate from his golden ceremonial goblets. In tropical America, where the cacao tree grows, the drinking of chocolate still has ceremonial importance. Long ago some Indian peoples used the fruit of the cacao tree to sue for the hand of a lady.

cocoa fruits

A young man would send some cacao beans, enough to serve at a party, to the girl of his choice. If he was accepted, a party followed and she would send him enough cacao beans for two parties. One party was to be held at the home of his parents, the other at her home, and there was sure to be a wedding. To this day it is a Latin-American custom at wedding receptions to serve chocolate to the guests.

Cacao beans have a chemical in them that gives us a temporary increase in energy. The coffee plant has such a chemical too. In ancient times, a brew of coffee leaves was used to reduce tiredness. There is an old story that coffee beans were first used by a monk living in a monastery in Arabia. One day while he was herding his goats he noticed that they suddenly seemed very frisky. He checked on what they had eaten and found that they were feeding on the beans of a coffee tree. Later he tried a brew of these beans himself. They kept him wide awake when everybody else around him was sleeping.

Although this story is supposed to have happened in Arabia, coffee came originally from northern Africa. It was taken to Arabia about five hundred years ago, and Turkish

coffee berries

merchants introduced it to Europe. In 1714, the mayor of Amsterdam gave Louis XIV a gift of a small coffee plant. It was so precious that the king gave it to the most celebrated botanist of his court to take care of. Nine years later rooted pieces of stem from this tree were put on a ship bound for the French colonies in the New World. The trees grown from these cuttings are said to have been the beginning of the whole coffee industry in America. Now Brazil is the world's chief coffee producer.

Coffee trees have glossy leaves and, when in flower, are covered with sweet-smelling white blossoms. These blossoms ripen into pulpy fruits, each one containing two coffee beans.

7 | The Grains We Eat

The cereal grains we eat, such as wheat, corn, and rice, are fruits that are of very special importance to people all over the world. Though we don't think of them readily as fruits, they do fit the scientific definition. Each grain is the developed ovary of a wheat, or corn, or rice flower.

Since ancient times man has depended on these nourishing grains for food. The first great civilizations in the valleys of the Nile, Tigris, and Indus Rivers depended on wheat and barley. The main food plants of ancient Greece and Rome were wheat and barley too. In the Far East, rice has always been a basic food plant. The highly developed cultures that the Spanish explorers found on the American continent could never have existed without corn.

Long, long ago wheat was just one of the wild grasses that covered the earth. Sometime in the dim past people began to gather its grains for food. Much later they began to plant the grains to get new crops of wheat. It is hard to know exactly how long ago and just where this happened, but we do know that wheat was being planted long before people invented writing, about six thousand years ago.

Archaeologists have also found actual grains of wheat

and barley in the remains of Egyptian settlements that are about seven thousand years old. Loaves of wheat and barley bread four thousand years old were found at one ancient site in Egypt. Carvings on the walls of early Egyptian tombs show how the wheat crop was sown and harvested.

In the valleys of the Tigris and Euphrates Rivers in Asia, archaeologists have found wheat and barley grains six thousand years old. They have also uncovered evidence in the ruins of ancient cities in the Indus River valley in Pakistan that wheat and barley were being planted and grown there, too, more than six thousand years ago.

Greece and Rome are ancient civilizations to us, and yet by the time they flourished the cultivation of wheat was so old that its origin was shrouded in mystery. The Greeks and Romans supposed wheat to be a gift of the goddess Ceres. The word *cereal* comes from her name.

For thousands of years, wheat was planted and gathered by hand. Gathering it was a long, difficult task. The wheat had to be cut and the grains beaten out of the wheat stalks. Then the grain kernels had to be separated from the parts around them, called "chaff." Usually this work was done by tossing the grain and chaff into the air so the wind carried the lighter chaff away from the heavier grains.

-Today we harvest our wheat crop with combines— giant machines that go through the wheat fields, cutting down the grain, separating it from the straw, or stalk, and from the chaff, and cleaning it. All these steps are done by one machine as it works through the field, and the golden grain is poured into bags or into trucks that take the grain to the flour mills. With this giant movable factory, eight men can harvest more than a hundred acres of wheat a day.

At the flour mill, the grains are ground into the flour that makes our bread. A wheat grain is white inside and brown outside. When the whole kernel—the brown coat of the seed and the white insides—is ground up, we have whole-wheat flour. If only the white part of the grain is ground, we have white flour.

A wheat plant looks like grass. Its leaves are long and narrow like those of other grasses, and its flowers are tiny and crowded together in long clusters at the top of the wheat plant. Each little wheat flower is very simple. It has three stamens, which bear the pollen, and one pistil. There are no petals—just little green sheaths around the stamens and pistil. When the pollen of the stamens is light and dry and ripe, it showers down over the pistil. The pistil has little feathery ends that stick out and help catch the pollen. After pollination, the ovary at the bottom of the pistil starts to swell. As the single seed grows inside it, the wall of the seed becomes joined to the ripening ovary wall and forms the grain, or fruit, of the wheat plant. The grains ripen together on the cluster at the same time, turning from green to golden yellow. In fact, the whole plant turns yellow as the grains ripen. Then the time has come for the cutting and harvesting of the wheat.

The food content of each wheat grain is starch and protein. If the wheat grain is planted, the young plant uses this food in the first few days of its life, before leaves are formed. If the wheat grains are not planted but harvested, we use this same starch and protein as food for ourselves.

Barley and rye and oats and rice are all fruits of grasses too. In each of them, the grains are formed in the same way as those of wheat. They grow from the ovaries of the pistils of the tiny flowers. Like wheat, they only plump out into grains after they are pollinated.

Barley, rye, and oats never became as important to man as wheat. Nevertheless, their grains have been used as food for a long time. Barley, whose original home was Ethiopia, is as ancient as wheat. Rye and oats were grown later in the history of civilization. Rye is a tough, hardy plant that withstands cold better than wheat does. Scientists think that rye came to be used in cold climates, where this grass grew as a weed and survived in wheat fields that failed to make a crop. Rye grains are dark, and the flour from them makes a heavy black bread, very popular in northern Europe.

Barley and oats are not used very much today, but people like barley soup, children love oatmeal, and horses still eat oats.

Rice is as important to people living in the Far East as wheat is to the other half of the world. Like wheat, it was cultivated long before history was written down. It was probably first grown as food somewhere in the tropical, marshy country of Southeast Asia. In both India and China, it has been the staff of life for thousands of years.

Unlike the other cereal grains, rice grows best in flooded land. Either natural rainfall or water brought by irrigation ditches from rivers and lakes supplies the plants with water. When the grains begin to ripen, the water is drained off, the ground hardens, and the crop is harvested.

The peoples of the Old World had cultivated wheat, barley, rye, oats, and rice since ancient times, but they did not know about Indian corn, or maize, until after America was discovered. Until then this giant grass was used as food only on this continent.

wheat

barley

rice

oats

Corn was the most important food plant grown by the ancient civilizations of America. Christopher Columbus was the first European to see it, when he landed in the West Indies in 1492. Magellan found it at Rio de Janeiro, and other explorers found it elsewhere in South America. In Peru, the palace gardens of the Inca Indians were decorated with images of corn in gold and silver. The golden ear of corn was shown among broad leaves of silver, and light tassels of silver floated gracefully from the top. Pictures of corn, woven into textiles and modeled on pottery, have been found in ancient Peruvian tombs. Even dried ears of corn were found in these tombs.

Explorers of the North American continent also found corn wherever they went. DeSoto saw it growing everywhere along his route from Florida and Alabama to the upper part of the Mississippi. Champlain first saw it in New England, and Miles Standish found corn when he was exploring for the Pilgrims.

Not all of the corn the explorers and early settlers found here was the same; there were many different kinds. There was hard corn and soft corn, flint and dent corn, popcorn and sweet corn, yellow, red, black, white, and many-colored corn. There was corn of many different shapes. Because all of these kinds of corn were already in existence when America was discovered, it is hard for scientists to unravel the history of this plant.

No one knows what the ancestor of the corn plant was really like. Plant scientists have traveled all over South and North America looking for its wild ancestor, but none has been found yet. Many plant breeders, who have tried to figure out the kind of plant it must have been, were delighted

Peruvian jug over 1000 years old

when an archaeological expedition found hundreds of corn-cobs and kernels in a cave in New Mexico in 1948. The scientists believe that the cave must have been lived in from 2000 B.C. to A.D. 1000 (about one to four thousand years ago). The oldest specimens of corn, found six feet under the soil in the cave, turned out to be a primitive kind like the one the plant breeders had suggested as the ancestor of the plant. Here is an example of the way two entirely different branches of science may produce evidence of a plant's history that fits together.

The Indians of our Southwest still grow many different kinds of corn. Some of their corn is starchy and easily ground into flour. Some is colored and used mainly as a source of dye for baskets and cloth. Some of it is the same sweet corn we eat. Corn is the mainstay of their life. Practically every meal includes corn in some form—cornmeal soups and mushes, cornmeal cakes known as tamales, or thin pancakes of corn-meal known as tortillas. It even serves as dessert in the form of popcorn sweets.

In our own corn belt in the Midwest, the field corn, grown in fields that stretch for miles and miles, has a same-ness about it that is astounding. Plant breeders have created a new variety of corn named hybrid corn. Fields of hybrid corn ripen at the same time, grow to about the same height, and form ears of corn about the same size at the same level from the ground. As a result, power machinery can go through a field and pick off the crop quickly and easily.

The sweet corn that we eat is only a small part of the corn crop grown in this country. Most of it is field corn, which is used to feed cattle and pigs. When we eat bacon and ham and beef, we are eating food from animals that depend on the waving fields of corn throughout the Midwest. The candy we eat has corn sugar in it. We use cornstarch puddings, corn flakes, corn syrup, and corn oil. The plastic industry also uses by-products of the corn plant. And today lots of our antibiotics, like penicillin, are grown in water in which corn has been soaked.

Have you ever seen a corn plant grow? When it first comes out of the ground, its leaves are wrapped together in a roll. As the stalk gets taller and taller, the long, narrow leaves spread apart and get bigger and bigger. Soon brownish tassels appear at the top of the main stem. These tassels carry only male flowers that produce pollen. If you look at a single flower in the tassel, you will see anthers hanging down. Dusty yellow pollen forms inside each anther, sifts

tassels of male corn flowers

out when the wind blows, and floats over the corn plants nearby.

Lower down on the plant ears form. The ears are made up of female flowers that grow together on the cob.

Each young ear of corn is made up of little pearly kernels arranged in rows on the cob, each kernel representing the ovary of a female flower. Long, silky threads, each one attached to an ovary, or kernel, lie over the rows. Every single kernel on the cob has its own silky thread, which sticks out through the top of the ear. There it catches the

corn ears made up of female flowers

pollen that drifts to it from the tassels of the nearby corn plants.

When a pollen grain lands on the silk, it sends out a tube that grows down inside the long, fine thread until it reaches the ovary. The contents of each pollen tube join with an ovule. This process fertilizes the ovules so they can develop into plump, yellow corn kernels. If a kernel is not fertilized, it remains small and underdeveloped, and we say that the corncob has grains that are not all filled out.

People need corn for food. They gather the grain and

kernels of corn on the cob

plant it. They cultivate the corn plants and pull the weeds from around them. They have made corn into a fine food crop. Although corn was once a wild grass, it has been so changed by cultivation that it can no longer grow without human care. If corn grains do drop off the cob and start to grow by themselves, they are soon crowded out by weeds. Left to itself, a corn plant would last about a year; then it would be blotted out by the stronger, tougher weeds.

People have also changed the other plants we eat. Our prehistoric ancestors may have discovered every important food plant long, long ago, but the plants they gathered looked very different from the ones we raise. We eat the plants we eat today because for thousands of years people have selected and cultivated the kinds of plants that suited their taste.

Index

*indicates
illustration

About the Author

Millicent E. Selsam's career has been closely connected with biology and botany. She majored in biology and was graduated magna cum laude with a B.A. degree from Brooklyn College. At Columbia she received her M.A. and M.Ph. in the Department of Botany. After teaching biology for ten years in the New York City high schools, she has devoted herself to writing. The author of more than eighty science books for children, Ms. Selsam has received the Eva L. Gordon Award of the American Nature Study Society, the Thomas Alva Edison Award, two Boys Club of America awards, and the nonfiction award for the Total Body of Creative Writing given by the Washington Children's Book Guild in 1978. In addition, she is a fellow of the American Association for the Advancement of Science.

At present, Ms. Selsam lives in New York City and spends her summers on Fire Island, New York.

About the Photographer

Jerome Wexler was born in New York City, where he attended Pratt Institute. Later he studied at the University of Connecticut. His interest in photography started when he was in the ninth grade. After service in World War II, he worked for the State Department in Europe as a photographer. Returning to the United States, he specialized in photographing advanced farming techniques, and the pictures he made have been published throughout the world. Since then he has illustrated a number of children's books with his photographs of plants and animals.

At present, Mr. Wexler lives in Madison, Connecticut.